Foreword

The ultimate guide to breeding and w
knowledgeable book, covering all asp
dog to breeding and whelping. This book stands out from a..,
others currently published by explaining in depth about
development, nutritional requirements, anatomy, birth defects,
illnesses, and fertility. The author hopes to fill the minds of male
and female dog owners with guidance and support in every way
possible from knowledge gained in running a k9 fertility clinic
herself and years of breeding experience first-hand, helping
poorly and sick puppies. The book is dedicated to the female
alone so each individual reader, both breeders and pet only
homes can get the maximum enjoyment by gaining knowledge on
buying, raising and behavioural training. The author struggled
with an accidental litter many years ago and found no help and
truly little advice on specific subjects so the idea of the book is the
help others who may experience the same, or a comparable
situation for which they can fully prepare. Since then, the author
now runs a successful k9 fertility clinic in the hometown of
Middlesbrough UK, helping people with advice, hand rearing
litters, helping with whelping females and works around the clock
building a reputable business clientele on all social media
platforms with top star reviews. The ultimate guide to breeding
and whelping offers a dictionary of technical terms in the back of
the book to help people understand what a vetinary practise has
explained to enable you to understand completely what has been
said in a simple, more understandable way. Each section of the
book provides in depth information of the cause, the treatment
and the recovery in defects, abnormalities and health conditions
that may arise throughout a female's life with her owner.
Regardless of breeding your female, the book will help with any
medical or health problems, training advise, feeding and
managing your female so you can both get the most pleasure
from each other. The author has explained in depth from buying a

female puppy, to then raising her puppy's litter from experience, with aftercare on the whelping mother and puppy developments in stages.

Introduction

As a dog owner, you may have thought about having puppies or breeding your male or female companion, but not sure where to even begin. The following book provides an in depth and detailed insight into dog fertility, breeding, whelping and all the parts in between to provide owners the knowledge and confidence to raise a happy and healthy litter of their own successfully. The world of breeding is a minefield, with so much to learn and research before even thinking about rushing into having a litter, hopefully this book is all you need as your guide. Breeding a litter of puppies is the best, most rewarding experience for anyone, but to see your female bring life into the world is extra special, as well as time consuming, costly, and very tiring. Reading The ultimate guide to breeding and whelping will make the experience a lot more enjoyable by being prepared and educated. I hope to fill the minds of dog owners with knowledge both researched and experienced direct to make the whelping experience enjoyable. I have authored the book in a certain way, simplifying terminology, which I think makes it easier for the reader to fully understand and learn from. The ultimate guide to breeding and whelping offers not only every aspect of breeding and whelping but also highly knowledgeable help and advice on puppy milestones, birth defects, diseases and difficulties that may arise as well as picking the correct stud for your female, using k9 fertility clinics and equipment you need to whelp a healthy litter. I hope that all the information needed is right here in this book to help you decide if breeding is for you and your female. Whether or not you decode breeding is for you or not I hope you are filled with the knowledge to help family and friends who may need assistance in the future. The book contains information regardless of breeding, including heat cycles, phantom pregnancies, having your female spayed and illnesses. Reading this book can give you the most pleasure from your female. Whether you have been breeding for years or just starting out this is always something to be learnt with research and experience no matter how long you have been breeding. Being able to recognise first hand your dog is sick, or something is wrong can save you time and your dog's life. Not only is the book knowledgeable for breeding and whelping, but it also helps you to understand behaviours and the anatomy of your female to give an understanding of what is happening on the inside of your female.

Obtaining a puppy

Before jumping in and buying the first cutest puppy you see, study the breeds you are interested in and make a list with other members of the family that live in the same household, so the breed of your choice is welcomed by everyone. Most people have a breed in mind to start off with, but often change their mind due to temperament, grooming needs, walking needs, it can become a dramatic family change. It is always best to get some first-hand experience with the breeds of your choosing before making any long-term commitments. Maybe visit animal shelters, rescue centres, friends and family who own the breed you are interested in, think about all the requirements your new puppy will need. Think about the space she will require and needs all year round, are you able to fit this into your current life. Research the breeds of your choosing to find out what problems they are commonly known for and any health testing that may need completing before breeding. Doing this will add onto the cost of your puppy so you can have an overall cost in mind. Researching breeds will help you in choosing the perfect breed for you and your family by breaking down breeds with health issues, breeds that suffer with

3

hereditary defects, or gain knowledge on how to help/make things easier if anything is to arise. When viewing a puppy, it is hard to stay calm and the possibility of saying no seems not an option, if something does not feel right, ask questions, and be prepared to walk away to think about it or refuse the puppy completely. Ask questions about how the mothers labour went, did she have a c-section? Are both dam and sire of the puppy health evaluated, has the puppy been health tested and does it have a vet health check record before leaving the breeder. The puppys mother (dam) should always be available to be viewed at the time of viewing the puppy, she should be in good health and the whelping area should be clean and not overly soiled with mess. If it is the first time you are buying a puppy, ask the breeder about Lucy's law and how they feel about a puppy coming back to them if its unsuitable in your home as life changes can happen meaning the puppy can no longer be housed with you. The breeder does have the right to refuse you your money back unless there was an underlying health issue. Under Lucy's law the breeder should always be offered the puppy back first before rehoming under 6 months of age to protect the puppy, the breeder is to make sure the puppy is in a suitable home. It is always good to have your new puppy checked over at the vets next available appointment to make sure the puppy you have bought is at a good weight, has no underlying health issues and is fit and well. If it was to arise that the puppy you have bought has a health problem or underlying condition, ask the vet to print off a copy of all documents noted and signed by both vet and new owner for you to hand over to the breeder, explaining the problem, the vet fees charged and any long term effects and medications needed as many breeders will always ask for evidence before taking the puppy back and refunding any money owed. Breeders often do not like having puppys returned and try to argue the case that the puppy was 'fine' when it left for their new home/collected, when in fact it has been sold with a heart murmur or defect. It is particularly important to buy your puppy from a reputable breeder to prevent any of this happening or make the process easier if it does arise, from a 'backstreet breeder who will argue their case. Be extremely cautious, especially if you are buying a male or female to use as a stud or to breed from, this can leave you with a puppy you love dearly, but cannot be used for breeding which was intended, it can leave you disheartened and angry. If you decide the puppy no longer fits into your home and family life after you have bought it, you should be able to return the puppy to the breeder depending on what contracts have been signed, with no money paid back to you. The breeder then will sell on to a more suitable home. The decision of whether to buy a puppy needs tremendous amounts of consideration and thought between the whole family. It is always best to buy a puppy when you and your family are settled in a home you plan to be in a long time, ensure you have the time and space, are comfortable with a job and money saved up for vet bills, also ensure you have the correct environment available to house a puppy so he/she can have the most stable and happy upbringing. There are many good reputable breeders which have waiting lists for puppys, so you have the option of putting your name down if you find the perfect breeder of your own chosen breed. Choosing to buy a puppy from a reputable breeder is good for everyone involved, they are well established, carry good bloodlines, puppys tend to come with health tests already conducted, DNA and temperaments are always brilliant as well as the breeder staying in touch. The breeder of your puppy should always be licensed to breed and sell puppys for all involved including the dogs, the breeder and the new owners so if there was a problem to ever arise the breeder is traceable and any information you would like to know you can stay in contact and ask if needed in the future. Many breeders like to see the puppy's they have bred be raised and grow up, it is a part of their legacy and breeding programme, also lovely to see their family's spoiling them, shows they have won, litters they have created and overall, how their lifestyle is. Be sure to ask the breeder of your new puppy what food she is currently eating so that you can have some prepared for when she comes home, as well as a crate (puppys like places they can have alone time and feel safe), ask if they are using puppy pads to urinate and poop on so you can continue to do so at home until she is house trained and learns to do her mess outside. Prepare your house for which room or area she will be in and set a crate/bedding area, ensuring they have plenty of warmth and nothing can bring danger to them by chewing, falling, or eating anything they should not that could be toxic or cause them to choke. Be sure to buy plenty of hard-wearing toys for the teething stage, which I call 'the worst stage,' puppys that are teething like to chew and bite anything and everything in their sight, including you, children, furniture, brickwork, plants, and anything left lying around. Cold carrots, toys, and plenty of chew aids like yaks or antlers are brilliant to have around the teething stage so you can distract them away from chewing other things with a substitute in place. Puppies are fed four smaller meals spread out over the day unlike older dogs, they have two main meals per day. The food you choose to feed your puppy should be of superior quality that provides a highly nutritional meal packed with the adequate vitamins and minerals to support growth and development. Once you have decided where the puppy's crate/bedding area will be, most people use the kitchen area, make sure the bed area is shaded from full sun (although dogs do love to have slight sunbathing spot), be sure it is a warm enough area all times of the day and night as she will spend a lot of time in the area sleeping. Puppies on average sleep for 12 hours per day. Puppies need alone time, time to get used to being left without their owners as puppy's can get separation anxiety. Try and be available to leave the puppy on her own for a little while, even if it is into another room to clean, with each time you leave your puppy leave her a bit longer, so she learns to settle and comfort herself. You will have to make some adjustments to your home, like having a child, move all medications or cleaning equipment up high so they cannot break into them and digest anything toxic that can be life threatening. Baby gates are good for keeping puppies to one room, or sectioning parts of your house to keep the puppy out, if the baby gates are fitted and installed properly, they bring no danger. When puppys leave their littermates they must feel lost and alone when staying in a new home with new surroundings with new people to adjust to, not to mention they will be extremely nervous and possibly a little scared, try to keep your routine normal and calm, giving your new puppy chance to explore their new surroundings and get used to her new family home. Your new puppy will take time to settle on a night crying and wanting to escape to explore, but good routine and leaving them cry is how they learn the routine of sleeping and when its bedtime in your home. The first few weeks after bringing your new puppy home is the hardest but they do get better with age and plenty of training which should be started immediately after entering your home. Good manners in a dog are always learnt from an early age to get the best temperament from your puppy that continues to adulthood as they know no different always being learnt what is good behaviour and what is not. When your puppy comes to you, they should have had their first vaccination, which will be on a vet card, it is your responsibility to have the second vaccine administered on time. Second vaccinations are usually due two to four weeks after the second, depending on the area, your chosen vet, and the injection type used which will protect them against parvovirus, distemper, leptospirosis, and parainfluenza. Getting your puppys second injection is especially important for her socialisation as she cannot go outside on the ground until she is fully covered and both vaccines have been administered. Socialising your puppy with other dogs, people and children is particularly important from an early age so they do not become aggressive and get used to being in social situations, also so they can understand and learn how to behave well practicing good manners in all areas and socialised places. Be sure to introduce your puppy to all aspects of life as early as possible like car journeys, walking near road sides (on lead), teaching to stop and sit or wait before you cross, take her to parks and social events where there is lots of noise and plenty of things going on but always have your new puppy on a lead, teaching her to walk neatly by your side. Training on a lead can be frustrating for the first couple of weeks with the pulling, excitement and many pups refuse to walk at all at first until they get used to walking outside which can take plenty of time and a lot of training with treats. Puppys need worming at 2, 4, 6, 8, 10 and 12 weeks, then every month or three-monthly intervals for the rest of their life depending on which brand you choose to use. Worming keeps your puppy healthy and clear of roundworms (Toxocara canis) which can affect puppy's growing in the uterus when breeding. It is always best to get your worming treatment from your vet that usually do package deals on flea and worming. Worming over 10-12 weeks will be administered as a tablet form rather than the puppys usual liquid or paste that the breeder will have given and should be easy enough to be given in a cheese or meat. You should always try to get your new puppy to take medications from your hand in case they are needed in future; it would be much easier than trying to hide medications in foods. It is always a good thing to have your pet insured, although insurance does not cover general vet bills like worming or general check-ups but used more for accidental emergencies like breaking a leg or an illness that arises as vets take full payment upfront that can be extremely costly, your vet will contact your insurance company for payment. The first year of a puppy's life is said to be the most prone for accidents happening as your new puppy is very bouncy and playful as well as an explorer wanting to jump from heights and eat things that she should not that can be seriously life threatening. Most insurance companies can be found online where you can compare coverage and costs that is right for you and your own puppies needs which can usually be cancelled at any time. Your new puppy will be experiencing the scariest time of its life in the next coming weeks as you prepare to bring her home, seeing new people, having new surroundings and no littermates to feel safety. Your first few days of training should be recall, she needs to learn her name and that it is good to come to your when called, always rewarding with small treats, but not too many that may make her sick, you can also reward good behaviour with a stroke and 'good girl.' Start off with casual visitors so you can teach her not to jump up using a command that she will learn. Ask any visitors that do come into your home to not let the puppy jump up, pushing her down carefully whilst you say your command for 'down.' This helps your puppy to learn the boundaries are with everyone and not just the family that live inside the home with her. Always be there when you have friends and family around and you give the commands, this learns your puppy that you are the leader, and she follows your instructions. Your puppy will choose a person from your household who she will automatically go to, sit with, and lay with who they will see as their leader, it may be that they find their voice soothing and comforting. In the first few weeks of your puppy being in her new surroundings try to keep voice levels nice and calm, shouting and screaming makes a puppy confused and scared, she may not know how to react, but do be sure to carry out normal day to day activities like hoovering and cleaning so they can get used to normal day to day household noises.

Owning a female

Females are considered easier than owning a male for many reasons, but there are also disadvantages the same for males' dogs, both have their advantages and disadvantages. Females are always smaller and lighter than the males of the same breed

9

because of their structure. Female dogs are less likely to roam or stray away from home unless they are in season (seeking a male). She is likely to be more settled than a male dog would be and affectionate as well as very loving. Females are easier to housetrain than males as they do not feel the constant urge to mark their territory unlike males. Females are well known to be easier to train, they become fully devoted to their owners and do anything to please them. Females are said to be a lot easier to train and are better than males at socialising and not forgetting females need more sleep than males, so they are asleep a lot longer. Females in season bleed, so they are highly likely to ruin furniture, it can be hard to maintain the cleanliness of your home for up to three weeks ever six to twelve months depending on when they cycle. She is subject to mood swings and behavioural changes when in heat/season. Many females will be eager to seek males when in season. Females have a higher level of PH in their urine which causes them to scorch grassed areas. Females may not be able to run as fast as males or be as agile. Females always cost more than a male because they are seen as worth more as you can breed from her. Females also tent to have more problems than males in terms of infections or if they need spaying it is a major operation. When planning to buy a dog, think about the sex of the dogs already in your household. A male and female housed together will always have to be separated completely whilst the female is in season (unless you are breeding), the male will stop eating, pine and cry all night and day. It is easier when owning both male and female to have one neutered or spayed or move one into a different home when her season is due to prevent the stress on both dogs and you as their owner. Think about family members or friends that visit with their dogs, are they friendly, your female's behaviour will change so she may become snappy around dogs she is usually lovely with. Visiting is best off being stopped with other dogs whilst your female is in season to protect both from harm and accidental pregnancy. It is almost impossible to keep an intact male and female away from each other in a communal household even when crates are used, they will burst out, or in some cases mate through the cage. Male and female dogs will always mate with their relations because they do not know or understand relations. Buying two female dogs can be an innovative idea because sisters are usually best friends and keep each other occupied without fighting, keeping each other company. Two puppies of the same age will be a lot harder to house-train instead of one single puppy alone to whom you can divide all your training attention. It is always best to leave it a few weeks or months between getting puppys so that the first is already trained in good behavioural and housetraining patterns for the second puppy to learn from. Females of the same age are highly likely to be in season at the same times each month and will synchronise together with each season at the same time with an age difference eventually. If you are wanting to breed, this means you would have two litters at the same time, two litters of puppies are a lot of challenging work and not enough sleep. Although the demanding work is endless, sometimes it is better to have two at the same time, especially if you have a waiting list for buyers. Having waiting lists can be particularly important to breeders, their litters are extremely planned and prepared so having potential buyers saves the emotional stress of being stuck unable to sell puppys. The older a puppy gets, the less likely you are to sell them at the original asking price, if anywhere near.

Knowing your female

When considering breeding your female there are many questions to answer first like how you must take her physical health into consideration. Can she walk well without breathing problems getting in the way? If she struggles to wall now, then think of how much she would struggle being pregnant and carrying the extra weight and strain of puppies. Some breed struggle more than others when they are pregnant, especially French bulldogs,

English bulldogs, and pugs, more often the flat nosed breeds. The extra strain of being pregnant can cause long term complications after the pregnancy and could be life threatening to mother and puppies. If your female is considered overweight or underweight, it is always best to get her to a healthy weight and condition before you consider breeding from her, which also applies if the mother has any sort of infections or having ongoing treatment, If any of the above do apply then it is always best to completely miss seasons until she is healthy. Unfortunately getting your female into a healthy breeding condition may never happen, all dogs are different, and the health of the dogs is always the highest priority over breeding. More often dogs have allergies to certain foods which the dog depends on injections to help ease the skin from hives and being itchy and the mother from pain and stress, these cannot be administered if the female is pregnant. Some dogs have problems like allergies, or medications and should not be used for breeding. Unfortunately, in our modern-day society these imitate licensed breeders and more often so, families are left devastated by their consequences.

Breeding

Before you consider breeding your female there are many options to consider first like is your female healthy, has she had the relevant health testing completed, do you have money put aside for whelping equipment and vet bills, money for continuous care for 8-12 weeks, is she mature enough, do you have the time and space for a litter, do you have a market to sell to and potential buyers ready?. The reason this question is asked is because dogs have become a huge market, with a lot of sold being sold to the wrong people and ending up left in kennels or rehomed. Once a dog is placed into kennels the longer, they are left their the less likely they are to find a long-term home. Some dogs are left in kennels that are long term residents and more likely to be euthanized. People do not see kennels as their go to for getting a dog because dog owners want to be able to raise the dog from being a puppy, so they have good manners, and the owner knows their temperament. Are you physically and emotionally ready to breed your female? The risks when breeding is potentially life threatening for your female dog and her puppy's. Some females have complications and can pass away during labour, puppy losses happen often as they get stuck in the birthing canal because they are too large to pass. Understanding when to intervene and get your whelping female to a vet is essential in caring for the whelping mother as complications do unfortunately arise if a whelping mother is left too long labouring. Loosing puppy's or even worse your female can be extremely hard on yourself and all the family. Do you have the time? Having time is crucial when it comes to thinking about having a litter from your female. Once your puppys are born, they need to be checked on at least every two hours including during the night and becomes round the clock care, so plan, take time off work, set a rota for members of the household to help, set out a timesheet of shifts beforehand to make sure you can do it. Having a litter can be physically and mentally exhausting, the thought of having puppies is ridiculously cute, but the work needed to go into having a litter can be time consuming, but worth the experience. Will you have transportation available for vet trips, checks and to get injections? There is much to consider before breeding your female which should be planned in every aspect to make it easier for yourself, your dog, and your family. Many people do not realise the work that is needed to go into breeding and raising a healthy litter and rush into it, thinking it is a quick money-making project. You should never breed for money alone, but to better the breed in which you choose.

Natural breeding's are not as common now because of the use of artificial insemination results, timing and cleanliness are seen as the go to option. A natural mating consists of the male dog mounting the female and penetrating the vulva whilst holding the female by her waist in position. Once the male is inside the vagina, he will then turn so they are in a bum-to-bum position. During this time, they are stuck together mating the male is leaking semen continuously, but the vigorous thrusting will have stopped and become more relaxed. The ejaculation process is split down into three different processes,' the first being the clear out of any urine from the penis, the second is the semen which is delivered in the first minute of penetration and the third is a considerable amount produced in the prostate gland which pushes the semen up to the oviduct. The semen then sits in the uterine tubes ready for the eggs to be fertilized. A tie from a natural mating can be timely and last anywhere from five minutes to one hour, sometimes even longer. This is also why artificial insemination is becoming more popular to reduce the timing of a natural tie. The tie will break apart on its own one the female releases the male's penis. Fluid will leak out of the female's vagina once the tie breaks apart, this fluid does not contain semen, but is the fluid that is released in the third stage from the prostate gland that flushes the semen to the cervix. During the tie ensure both stud and female owner are holding them into place by their collars so any breaking away, ripping and tearing can be avoided. The stud fee is usually paid upfront for his duties unless an agreement is put in to writing and signed by both male and female owners. Pup back deals on a stud dog is used on the terms a puppy is handed over instead of the upfront stud fee. By doing a pup back deal there are no upfront costs on artificial inseminations or mating's, but the puppy is sold at a larger cost than the stud asking price. Some studs offer this service to certain females to keep a puppy back for themselves to add to their breeding programme, especially if they have a high-quality bloodline. Two mating 24 hours apart at least in the minimum you should accept when breeding your female to secure the changes of your female falling pregnant, whether it be two natural mating's or two artificial inseminations'. Slip ties are known to

14

also get a female pregnant which is when the male penetrates the female's vagina but does not get stuck as a tie, but instead 'slips out.' Mating has a better chance of the female falling pregnant if the tie lasts around twenty minutes. It is wise to ask the stud owner before the mating goes ahead if they are willing to allow a free remating or artificial insemination on the females next season if she does not fall pregnant the first time, ensuring contracts are signed. A female owner is to pay stud for his duty only and not for a litter of puppies so a free remate is not always accepted, especially if the female is to absorb the litter because the stud had done his duties in getting the female pregnant, absorbing is down to the female.

Puppy absorption is when the foetuses disintegrate in the uterus usually from an infection a problem in the pregnancy. Puppy resorption usually happens before the puppy has any bone formation before day 45. Canine fetal resorption happens in at least 11% of all the female pregnancies. Although the chance of resorption is due to the female having an infection, there are also many other causes like genetics, nutritional factors, hormones, development, hypothyroidism, placenta/uterine anomalies, and medications given whilst pregnant. There is also research into environmental factors like where the dog lives and sleeps, the conditions of living arrangements, plug-in air fresheners, scented candles, smoking cannabis around a pregnant female, weather changes and any home moves due to stress. Infections causing puppies to absorb can be down to coli, brucella canis, canine herpes virus, parasites, streptococci, salmonella, pasturella and proteus. Because reabsorption can happen before a pregnancy scan, it can often be mistaken for being pregnant when in fact she is having a phantom pregnancy as they can still act like they are pregnant because of the hormones released. A female absorbing is a quite a common issue but not usually noticed by breeders or their owners and is unfortunately not preventable. If your female seems to absorb regularly then is would be best to speak to your vet as she may have some underlying health issues that prevent her from carrying a litter. Some females for instance for instance can be carrying a litter of eight confirmed puppys, but only four absorb and the rest are born happy and healthy with no underlying or present health issue. The foetus is absorbed back into the female's body, usually you do not see anything exit or blood show, but if a female is to absorb later in the pregnancy once the puppies have developed bones after day 45 then it is highly likely she will deliver them, but they will not be fully formed functioning puppies. Breeders often administer a course of antibiotics on the first day of the female's season and for 7-10 days to give the body a full flush out before they are mated to reduce the risks of puppy's absorbing in case there is an infection present but undetected.

Pregnancy

A females dogs pregnancy lasts nine weeks, on average that's 57-67 days, larger breeds tend to give birth earlier but most averaging 63 days from a natural mating or artificial insemination. For those 9 weeks the female body has remarkably similar hormonal and physiological changes like a human would, but each phase and change only lasts 3 weeks. Some dogs have a high a low tolerance to food, one day they will swallow it down hole then refuses to eat for two days. Most females also have behavioural changes, there are many different changes to your female's body inside and out for example: Appetite changes, behavioural changes, dislikes to food they usually like and opposite, loose stools, swelling of the vulva, affectionate, sleeping more often, being snappy towards other dogs, pining, pacing, and feeling down in themselves. Each female dog is different in pregnancy and breeds. Be sure to research your breed extensively before you begin the process. There are many different views on breeding especially when the best time/age is. Some breeders breed at 12 months old (most registrations will accept a 12-

month-old female), and some believe, like myself, that 18 months (or third season) is best as this age they have fully matured. You need to spend time with your female, get to know her, teach her good manners, and get her into a good routine before breeding. I think as a dog owner you know yourself if your female is mature enough, she will have settled down a lot from being a puppy or teenager, she will also be less active as she matures and has less energy to burn off. By 18 months of age, they are more ready to have a litter, they are less likely to absorb if she is less active, you will understand her temperament better than she was at 12 months, helping you with a major breeding decision knowing you have better understanding of her temperament. Is it a temperament you would have in a puppy? A female can have a litter every six months of age with each season, but this does not make it right and it should never be done in any circumstances not every season. Females need time to heal and rest after each litter because a female's uterus after having puppies takes twelve months to settle back to normal with added scar tissue after each litter, it is important to let them heal as during this time they become open to infections. Although there are no special dietary requirements during mating, it is sensible to adjust her food intake accordingly to maintain a healthy weight. It is good to monitor your female's weight beforehand, during and after pregnancy, during lactation. Feeding the correct diet during pregnancy is essential for breeding success and rearing a health litter. Most of the fetal growth happens in the third stages of pregnancy, when the food intake should be increased. Many people believe that increasing the food intake throughout the full pregnancy is needed but is it a myth and no increase should be given until the last 3 weeks of her pregnancy, although personal experience my females have always been slightly hungrier as early as day twenty-four. Feeding more throughout the full pregnancy can cause an unhealthy female that may struggle to whelp with the extra weight. Be sure not to overfeed to avoid complications in labour. The increased food given towards the end of pregnancy should be introduced slowly, starting with 10% more per week until 50% extra meal serving is gained. The females growing uterus takes up the extra strain in her abdomen, making it better if she is fed several smaller meals per day instead of fitting whole full meals in. Many owners like to supplement the pregnant female, but if she is fed a nutritional diet then no added vitamins or minerals are needed. Lactation is the most demanding part to satisfy, it must supply every puppy with the nutrition and everything they need to survive and thrive. After the third or fourth week depending on the litter size the female's food will need to increase by three to four times their maintenance allowance to keep the demand of the milk supply. Fresh drinking water should be available 24.7 throughout the full pregnancy. Females that have needed to have a C-section performed take longer to heal than those who have birthed natural because they have had major surgery and scar wounds have a large chance of becoming infected or tearing apart, which should be cleaned twice per day to help prevent a poor healing process. Some female dogs may not mature until they are two or three years old, only you and your vet can determine this as breeding too early will have complications but breeding too late can have worse complications. Breeding to late in a female's life can have life-threatening risks to carrying a litter and the birthing process especially past the age of six or seven. Most breeders retire their breeding females after five years old. Your female should be at a healthy maintained weigh for her breed, have no health problems, no current infections, or skin disorders, no hernias, or defects before your considering breeding from her. All the relevant health testing for her breed should be completed before breeding to ensure the best successful outcome of a litter and a health whelping mother. Pregnancy can be determined at 28-35 days after a natural mating or artificial insemination by an ultrasound technician who will perform an ultrasound scan at a k9 fertility clinic or vet. An experienced sonographer will be able to determine whether your female is pregnant by looking for foetuses and count the number they can see to give you an estimate litter number, but do know that ultrasound scans on dogs are only a rough estimate as some puppys can mirror image which can look like there is more puppys than what their actually is. There are many ways of detecting pregnancy also through changes in the body that include increased blood supply to the nipples, they will become pink and prominent, especially the ones closest to the hind legs as well as being fuller as the mother is preparing for the milk supply. A reliable Indication of pregnancy usually happens around day 26 and is a creamy coloured discharge from the vulva that should be odourless but is a particularly good sign your female is pregnant. Many females also have morning sickness, like a human that can happen anytime of the day, which is usually a yellow frothy bile type of sick and is nothing to worry about, unless she is being sick repeatedly or not eating at all then contact your vet as lack of nutrition to puppys can be life threatening, leading to absorption. This can happen if a female is refusing to eat or is being sick a lot more than usual, if a mother is not eating, the puppies are not able to get the vitamins and mineral for them to grow and form correctly, causing birth defects. When a pregnant mother reaches the morning sickness phase it is a suitable time to start introducing smaller, more frequent meals throughout the day, so her stomach is not overloaded all at once. Morning sickness is cause by the hormone changes and pressure of the uterus growing. Feeding time routines will be changing now she may start refusing foods she usually likes and eating at various times compared to her usual set mealtimes. Offer food little and often as a pregnant female's appetite changes you may find your female wanting four to six smaller portions throughout the day over her two set meals times. The stomach area getting larger is also a clear indication of the female being pregnant, although larger breeds do not start getting bigger until around six weeks unlike smaller breeds who can be showing a larger stomach at four to five weeks. Days 45-50 you can sometimes start to see foetal movement when the female is laid on her side, after a drink of cold water. During pregnancy, your females coat may start to change, getting thinner, bald patches or extreme hair loss especially after the puppies have been born due to hormonal changes and the puppies putting extra strain on the mother for nutrients. Be sure to help your females coat maintained by using soft brushes, making sure she is free from fleas and ticks. Never use a soap or wash on your females coat because she can lick this off and pass toxins on to her puppies, as well as making herself poorly by ingestion. Walking is still essential during pregnancy to stay healthy and active, but it is strongly advised not to walk your pregnant female (or any dog in this case) in warm/hot weather, but instead walking early morning or late afternoon once the sun is set to prevent sun stroke, dehydration, and heat exhaustion. Strenuous running, rope pulling, jumping, and climbing should be avoided completely to keep the puppies healthy and to prevent the mother from overstraining. It is always best to keep your pregnancy female on a lead and do small walks on paths, especially towards the end of her pregnancy letting her control the distance and speed, staying local to your home so you can get back quickly if needed. Some dogs, for instance working dogs still work until they are late in pregnancy, running around fields high-speed staying regularly active, it all depends on what your female is used to and how active she usually is. If your female is usually active, she is likely to stay active during pregnancy and slow down towards the end.

Phantom pregnancy

Females can have the same hormonal changes even if they have not been mated and are likely to experience at least one phantom pregnancy within their lifetime, some females will even have milk production and carry teddys around with them as puppy's, protecting and guarding them. A phantom pregnancy can often last up to three weeks, six weeks after her season began and no medical intervention is needed, although if it becomes intense your vet can prescribe a medication such as Finilac, which helps to dry the milk produced quicker so the female can return back to normal faster than she would with no medication before mastitis begins. There are many ways of helping a female during a phantom pregnancy like walking her more often than usual, having regular exercise at this time can help keep her mind occupied. Removing all teddies and toys away so she is not encouraged to treat them as puppys,' removing her bed during the day so she is not wanting to lay and sleep as often, reduce her water intake, and feed more carbohydrates. A phantom pregnancy can return with each season but do not have a litter just to satisfy your female as the phantom pregnancies will only get worse with each season ahead. If you decide that having a litter of puppies is not for you, the best option would be to have your female spayed to prevent the ongoing phantom's. During a female phantom pregnancy, she may become very needy/clingy, wanting to be with someone all the time for comfort, she may whine and cry because their hormones are up and down so they are left confused and often come withdrawn from day-to-day things they would usually enjoy. Removing any teddies or toys will help rid the phantom pregnancy sooner as she will see them as her puppys, wanting to carry them around and clean them. If the female is allowed her teddys it will keep her thinking she has given birth that will keep her lactating, producing milk. A female that is having a phantom pregnancy will try to lick her nipples often which will cause the milk flow to continue as this mimic the puppies suckling for milk, try to stop her anytime you can and avoid rubbing her stomach area completely until the phantom is over and her milk has dried up.

Heat cycles and ovulation

A heat cycle/season may last up to three weeks that starts with swelling of the vulva then a bloody discharge that is usually heavy and fresh red in colour for the first 6-8 days but as her heat continues, her blood will become lighter in colour and consistency as the process of heat continues. Other signs that your female is in season are nervousness, high-strung, pacing around, licking the genital area, all of which are completely normal, although she will want attention more than usual. Heat cycles vary with different dog breeds large and small, where some females will have heat cycles every six months to the date, others may have them every 8-10 months as well as some seasons being yearly, every 12 months for many females. Every female is different and may take some cycles before they regulate. On day 9-14 of your females season the blood will turn to a pink/salmon colour during her ovulation period but some can be shorter on longer depending on what stage of their heat they will ovulate. Never try to mask over a females scent of being in season, no sprays or powders offered on the current market will mask a female in season to a male dog and it may cause infections whilst the vulva is swelled, that may cause infections if anything were to get inside the vaginal area. A male dog will always know if a female is in season even if she is having a silent heat and no blood is present. During your females heat cycle she will ovulate, releasing eggs, ready for the male's semen to fertilize which usually happens around day 9-14 but can be earlier or later and is less common. The best way to determine when ovulation is occurring is by getting a cytology or progesterone test conducted at a k9 fertility clinic or your vet. Both methods are explained later in depth on how they are conducted and what they do. Stages of the oestrous cycle are split into segments of phases, each explained here:

Anoestrus

The anoestrus phase is the non-breeding portion of the cycle and is marked by inactive ovaries. A female is this stage will be attractive to male dogs but will not let them mount her and she may snap if a male is to try. The aggression shown is the female telling the male she is not ready to be mated or artificially inseminated.

Pro-oestrus

This phase is the beginning of your female's season. The vulva area will start to enlarge or may be already swelled before blood is seen. This phase of her heat she will produce red fresh blood that will be seen coming from the vaginal area. Although the female will be found attractive to male dogs, she will not accept a dog to mount her and may become aggressive to any that do try. She may become needy and sleep a lot more than usual due to hormonal changes in the body.

Oestrus

This phase is when the female will accept the male to mount her or be ready for the artificial insemination process to begin. Ovulation begins around two days before this phase so the eggs will be released ready for the male's semen to fertilize. The vulva will be very much enlarged, and her bleeding will have slowed down and changed from red to pink. The female will stand for a male present, pushing her bum in the air and putting her tail to one side for him to mount her.

Met-oestrus

This phase happens in the unmated females and hormone levels are the same as a female that would be pregnant. During this stage, the female may show signs of a false pregnancy known as a phantom pregnancy. She may produce milk in her nipples and carry toys around like they are puppys, along with behavioural changes.

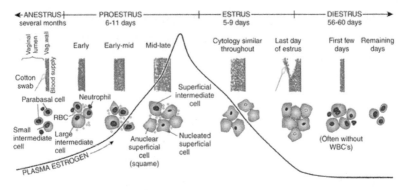

A dry season/absent heat is when a female has no bleeding at all and little or no swelling, this is known as an abnormality and happens particularly in larger breeds more than the smaller breeds. A dry season makes it harder for the owner to breed a female as your typical signs of a season are not there. The only way to achieve a pregnancy from a dry season is if both male and female live in the same household or progesterone blood tests are conducted every 2-3 days and daily once the numbers start to rise because they can double overnight to determine exactly when she is ovulating. Females in season often clean themselves so it is a good thing to write down and keep track of her seasons which will give you an idea of when her seasons are due. Absent heats can be confirmed by weekly progesterone testing or cytology so the owner can detect the LH surge ready for breeding.

A split season is when a female starts her heat but does not ovulate. Her season will begin the same as a normal season would with swelling on the vulva and bleeding. Split seasons are split into two heats weeks or months apart with the first part of the heat not progressing to the normal oestrus phase but instead the first part of her season ends. The second part of her season is when she will be able to breed and ovulate, releasing eggs for the semen to fertilize. Ovulation occurs as a normal part of her season in the second stage and usually happens in younger females caused by a lack of pituitary output of LH. The low levels of LH will not allow her ovaries to generate ovulatory follicles and serum progesterone will have an exceptionally low value, which stops the heat. Medication or treatment is not usually required as the females' heats should correct themselves as they mature with every season. If you find your female is having reoccurring split season it is best to speak to your vet who will give advice on how to correct it or treatments that are available and suitable for your female.

Silent heats are hard to detect from a human perspective. A female having a normal heat shows many signs like swelling of the vulva, bleeding and discharge unlike a silent heat that are barely visible, if anything at all. A female having a silent heat may show no interest at all around other male dogs unless they are at the stage of ovulation which usually leaves a week window for her eggs to be fertilized. Smaller breeds who reach sexual maturity earlier tend to have one or two silent heats before their heat cycles regulate. It is hard to determine when a female is bleeding sometimes, a lot of females lick themselves clean when they feel pooling blood at the vulva and lick up and drops that have dropped onto the floor. If you are wanting to breed a female whilst she is having a silent heat this is fine to go ahead with. Bringing the stud dog into contact with the female every few days to detect their behaviour which will help you determine optimal breeding times as well as conducting cytology and progesterone testing to be sure you do not miss her ovulation period.

Prolonged heats are when your female has a heat cycle that lasts longer than 3 weeks or 21 days and still shows signs of bleeding, swelling, appealing to males, and having discharge. Prolonged or ever shorter heats often happen during the first few cycles of a female's dogs' life, but everything regulates to normal after some heat cycles. The main cause for prolonged heat cycles is based on a hormonal dysfunction such as persistent elevation of estrogen that is caused by an estrogen-producing ovarian cyst or by granulosa cell tumor of the ovary. Ovarian tumors require surgery to remove it. Ovarian cysts need time to be monitored to see if they regress or not, if they do, surgery will be required. A cyst or tumor can be easily identified using ultrasonography by a vet. Prolonged heats can be terminated/ended a lot quicker by using the estrus suppression method that includes using mibolerone, an androgen preparation, which will be administered over a course of three or four months. Once your females heat is over, she will come into season again and will be able to breed with no complications. There is of corse the method of spaying to prevent a prolonged heat from happening again.

Prolonged interestrous interval is when a female has a normal heat cycle but then does not have one again until after sixteen months or more have passed. Highly likely the cause of this would be an ovarian cyst that starts to produce progesterone, a hormone like androgen, they both either stop or prevent a heat from happening. Conditions like cushings syndrome and hypothyroidism can generate long term anestrus. Hypothyroidism can be detected by a thyroid blood test conducted by a vet but cushings syndrome does not affect reproduction and the ability to carry a litter as it most commonly affects older females. Mixing females that have this problem with females that tend to cycle regularly without problems often helps the females synchronise with the other females that will help to correct the female's cycle. They may slowly become more appealing to males and regulate back to a normal fertility and season cycle.

When the female's body has not recovered properly from the progesterone induced damage, the mucus membrane lining the womb is not hormonally receptive to embryo-implantation making it extremely hard for the female to fall pregnant. For older female dogs who have short interestrous intervals, your vet may suggest using androgen to supress the current or next upcoming heat before ovulation, so the endometrium has enough time to recover until the next heat. Androgen is not usually offered to younger females as explained, they usually have a few heats until their cycle regulates so no intervention is needed unless it becomes a reoccurring problem.

Vaginal cytology and progesterone testing

Vaginal cytology can be performed to determine the optimum time to breed and enhance the success of pregnancy by telling you when she Is ovulating or when she may ovulate. This process may need repeating to determine the correct time for mating or artificial insemination, so the male does not miss the female's ovulation window. The process needs repeating if she is early into her season or if she is far off from ovulation. Vaginal cytology being performed should not hurt or cause any distress to your female and should take no longer than 60 seconds to get a good sample/swab. The types of cells show above present themselves under a microscope depending of the stage of estrus she is at. Vaginal cytology is performed by taking a swab of the vaginal wall, coated onto a small glass slide with dye to optimise the cells present, and put under a microscope for examination which the results are instant. Progesterone testing is displayed in numeric format, usually ng/mL and nmol/L using a machine to determine whether the female is a peak ovulation for breeding. These exact numbers are used when traveling to breed, or the stud is traveling to you. Progesterone testing is also used when using frozen or chilled semen to ensure it is put into the female at the correct time and eliminates the risk of traveling and her not accepting the male to mount her or mate, although frozen and chilled semen is artificially inseminated so that is only if traveling for natural mating's. Progesterone testing involves getting a sample of blood from the female's vein (usually in the front legs) by a vet, separating the serum from the plasma through a spinning machine, and then onto a sample and into the progesterone

27

machine that then gives an automatic printed result once complete. The test results are available in 15-30 minutes depending on what type of machine is used as there are many different types that can run quicker than others. Progesterone testing is mostly conducted when the stud fee is a large amount of money so the risk of the female not falling pregnant is unlikely, unless there is an underlying problem with the female. Vaginal cytology is seen as a budget alternative to progesterone testing, but I have found personally running a k9 fertility clinic that people like to use cytology, until close to ovulation, then use progesterone to be sure she is ovulating by the cytology results. Progesterone testing is more expensive than cytology, so it keeps the overall cost down and the need to take blood from your female more often than needed.

Male dogs and stud support

Male dogs are usually sexually producing semen at 6-8 months of age, but this does not mean they should be producing litters or evening thinking about being used to a stud dog just yet. Responsible breeders should wait until a male dog is 18 months of age at least and in larger breeds they may not be fully matured until 24 months old with all the relevant health tests completed before seeking females. Waiting allows you as an owner to ensure he is healthy. Mature, fully grown and his temperament should be fully recognised that can be passed down to any offspring produced. Relevant tests are different in several types of breeds with many health screening schemes that can be conducted to ensure superior quality traits are passed down. Health testing includes hips and elbow dysplasia scoring, deafness testing, eye screening, inbreeding calculators, and respiratory function grading. Assessing your dog for all of these gives you a better understanding of what your dog may or may not pass on to future offspring and gives you the information required to avoid producing puppies with health issues and defects. Selecting males and females for breeding that have had all their relevant health testing completed gives you a clear understanding of what will complement your male or female to reduce the risk of diseased producing in future generations. Breeding decisions should always be well balanced, take into consideration the qualities and how compatible the mating will be including temperament, genetic diversity, and the general health of both dogs. This about the structure and quality overall for instance, if your female has a short nose/flat face and often struggles on long walks you need a male that has a longer snout and open nostrils to correct the problem which makes for better breeding. This applies to all brachycephalic breeds, especially French and English bulldogs that are currently taking over the market with new crazes implementing big ropes and fluffy bulldogs. Always think of a vison you want to create that betters the breed in all aspects down to breathing, structure, temperament, health, and DNA. A semen test can be conducted at a k9 fertility clinic that will check the viability of the male dog's semen ensuring it is healthy enough to use when breeding. Some male dogs have extremely healthy semen whilst others may be inadequate quality or nothing at all. Semen evaluation depends on how old the male is, if hes been used as a stud dog before, whether he is mature enough, if there is a female present at the time or extracting the semen and he may be too old or too young to produce anything. Many factors help to make the process easier for the male dog to produce at the time of the semen collection for the sample to be assessed. Semen testing has become extremely popular with the growing market and is quite easy for a k9 fertility clinic to conduct. A collection sleeve is placed around the penis with added pressure to the bulb encouraging an erection the male will then start to thrust, especially if a female is present which will produce semen into the sample bag. An exceedingly small sample of semen is syringed up and placed onto a glass slide with a very thin glass slide over the top, the glass slide is then placed under the microscope and examined by the fertility clinic. A semen test shows instant results which both clinic owner and customer can see on a screen. Performing a semen test of a male dog causes no harm to the male dog and should not cause any distress although lubrication can be used to help the penis retract back into the prepuce sheath as sometimes the male can thrust too hard, causing the skin to push back too far which can cause the male slight discomfort. It is always best to study the breed of your choosing to discover their family heritage, so you understand what they have to offer in terms of colours they carry and bloodlines. A stud dog is usually a registered full breed with papers and health testing complete. Breeding a male dog after 8 years of age is usually frowned upon because of health deteriation and inadequate quality or lack of semen produced, some males are stopped working at five years of age. It is good to have your male's semen regularly evaluated when using him as a stud dog to ensure it is of good breeding quality. Both sire and dam (male and female) should be up to date on all vaccinations before considering a breeding pair. As a stud owner it is your responsibility to make sure your male has regular health and semen checks, making sure to take him off the stud market if an infection arises until it has cleared up and been medicated or if he has poor semen quality.

Equipment, labour, and whelping

A whelping box is essential when breeding, somewhere your female is happy, warm, and content when having her puppies that should be large enough for mother and all puppies, but not too large or the mother may stand on them. Introduce your whelping box one or two weeks before your female is due to go into labour so she can familiarise herself with her new surroundings and get used to her new bedding area (if different to usual). The whelping box should have pig rails/guardrails around the sides to prevent

30

puppies from being laid or stood on, gloves for handling new-borns or assisting with the whelp, clean towels to rub the puppies down when they exit and to keep her whelping area warm, bedding is essential to keep puppy's warm as well as sheets and blankets, you can never have too many as the bedding area will need changing regularly to keep it clean and free from infections. Rubbing new-born puppies with towels helps to stimulate their organs and to help rid of any fluid they may have ingested when exiting the birth canal. Be sure to have a car available with plenty of fuel in case of needing an emergency trip to the vets incase complications do arise so you can get there quickly. Have your vet's number to hand and prices wrote down, opening times and out of hours services to make it quicker for yourself and the whelping mother to get there instead of rushing around trying to find a vet that is open if out of hours are needed. A nasal aspirator is needed for puppies born with fluid in their mouth, chest, or lungs, this enables you to suction any excess fluid from the nose and throat. Unscented/unwaxed dental floss is used to tie the cords if the whelping mother needs assistance. Heating pads, heat lamp and/or a hot water bottle as puppies need to stay warm during the first weeks of their lives as they cannot regulate or keep their own body temperature, so warmth is particularly important to maintain organ function. Round tipped sterile scissors are used so you can assist the female if needed in cutting the puppies umbilical cords if needed because sometimes puppies can be delivered too quick for the whelping mother to do them on time themselves. Adjustable puppy ID collars helps with identifying puppies as some will come out looking the same for instance German shepherds and rottweilers. By using puppy ID collars, you can identify a puppy that may need extra help with feeding or assistance with care. Keep a pen and paper handy ready for the birth keeping accurate readings of times puppys were born, the gender, and most importantly their weight gain throughout the eight weeks to ensure they are healthy and gaining weight. It is always good to have a milk supplement prepared and bottles available in case a puppy needs extra help with feeding or the mother needs help if she has had a large litter to make sure each puppy is having regular fluid intake. Liquid calcium, vanilla ice cream and cottage cheese is beneficial for a whelping mother as labour can make her calcium levels drop which causes behavioural changes such as snapping at her puppies or growling, she may shake or become stressed continuing to dig her bedding area up. By administering a form of calcium, it can help the mother release the parathyroid hormone from her bones that give her the power to push stronger and longer. Oxytocin can be administered after a puppy is born to help a whelping mother build stronger contractions for pushing and can be administered in 30-minute intervals, but never before a puppy is born as it can also stop contractions and labour. Oxytocin is administered when uterine inertia begins to develop, before the contractions stop completely which is a hormone used to increase uterine contractions that helps a whelping mother push her puppy's out. A thermometer is also a good piece of equipment to have to monitor the female's temperature so you have an idea of when labour will begin. Taking a female's temperature and monitoring her levels a week before her due date will give you an idea of when labour will begin once the 'temp drop' is seen. A drop in temperature means labour will start within 24 hours. The normal temperature of dogs will range from 37.8 (roughly) and will drop to low 36 for example 36.1-36.5 for a few hours before spiking back up to the normal range, meaning labour is not far away. This temperature drop method and reverse progesterone testing is the only method dependable to detect labour. Reverse progesterone testing is very much the same as progesterone testing for ovulation but it is read in a different way for instance, the numbers read below 5 means the pregnant female is ready to give birth soon or is viable to be opened up for a c-section unlike a progesterone reading at 38nmol would mean she is ovulating and ready for her first mating or artificial insemination to take place. Keeping your females whelping are clean, comfortable, and warm is extremely important when raising a litter to prevent bacteria and infections from growing and spreading. Stock up on dog friendly cleaning supplies as well as baby wipes, tissues, gloves, and lots of bedding. Once the puppies are 3-4 weeks old the weaning process should begin, starting off with puppy mouse or dry food softened in hot water (do not feed until cooled. The weaning stage is extremely messy so have all your cleaning supplies easily accessible for yourself but not the mother. You should never separate a mother from her puppy's but unfortunately that is sometimes out of your hands. Puppies should only be removed from her mother if she is injured, or any littermates need hand-rearing. Separating a puppy from its mother before they are weaned fully onto food can lead to many problems including behavioural issues, separation anxiety and poor health. Removing the puppies from the mother can cause her extreme amounts of stress which can cause her loss of appetite that is not good as she needs to eat for nutrition and for milk supply to her puppy's. a mother's instinct is remarkably like a human, we become protective, we know when our children are hurt or in distress the same as a whelping female, she will become very protective of them all. Removing the puppies from the mother at six to eight weeks to allow for a developed immune system, social development, and anxiety as well as bite regression, learning to cope without their mother and preparing for their new homes. A whelping mother should never be separated from her puppies to ensure they do not dehydrate, stimulation to toilet is necessary to prevent a ruptured bladder and constipation. If the mother is not licking them to stimulate them to toilet, try holding the puppy's near to her mouth to show her what to do but you can also use a non-scented baby wipe to mimic the mother licking them. A mother who has recently had a litter of puppies will become very protective of them and may not let family members go near them. Your female will not understand you or other family members are only there trying to help her and not to hurt them, she may see people as a threat. Each whelping mother is different and takes to birthing and having puppies differently. It is best not to allow visitors even though it is an extremely exciting time for everyone, but visitors can bring in many germs and infections on their hands and feet so keep it minimal, use pictures and videos to send instead of people physically entering your home. Being there to support your female in labour is important, but also try not to be too involved, give the whelping mother a chance to open the sacks surrounding the puppies and bite the cord first, making sure she does not bite too far down. If a mother is to chew to cord too far it can lead to a hernia from pulling of the muscles when the mother is chewing. Females that are whelping are all hugely different, some females may need their owner remarkably close by at all stages of labour, some females may not want anyone they are at all and will not go in to labour until she is on her own and comfortable. However, your female likes to labour, be sure to be always close by in case you do need to intervene. Many owners find use of buying a camera, this way you can see her if you leave the house on the weeks leading up to labour, watch back on the birth of her labour and watch the puppies growing.

Giving birth

All females' labours are different, especially times of delivery. Some females can take 24-36 hours, even longer depending on the females age, health and how well their labour progresses. Most females give birth with no complications, but they do arise, and you should be prepared for any outcome that may happen. Once the temperature has dropped, labour will be within 24 hours. Now is your time in the present moment to make sure everything is ready and prepared for the upcoming labour, so everything is easily accessible. The foetuses start the onset of labour, once they are crowded in the uterus which stimulates the immature cardiac and respitory systems, ready for the dramatic changes ahead. During this time, your female will be off her food and may not eat for 24 hours before labour starts, until labour is complete. She will be restless but deep sleeping a lot throughout the day when she is usually awake, she may spend a lot of time digging and scratching at her bed making a nest for her puppies, you can give her newspaper or blankets just for this purpose, so she feels she is accomplishing her task of creating a safe environment. Sickness is common and completely normal when your female is in labour as her contractions get stronger, she will start to pant excessively from the stomach. Be sure to always have plenty of fresh drinking water available and be easily accessible for her to get to as she can dehydrate quickly. It is important to keep your female hydrated so she has energy when the pushing stage arrives. Just before whelping your female will lose her mucus pug that protects the cervix, or it may have come away over the weeks/days leading up to labour and will look like a stringy, clear discharge coming from the vulva as her body prepares for labour. Once the onset of labour has begun, fluid will leak out of her vagina in different colours with a bloody tinge as her contractions get stronger and the puppies are entering the birth canal. In the first stages of labour the cervix should have dilated to allow the puppies to push down from the uterus and be born, the foetus must rotate headfirst for a safe delivery. If a puppy becomes stuck, contact a vet immediately as this can become life threatening for both the mother and her unborn puppy's, especially the ones that are stuck behind one that is stuck, it is classed as a blockage. One the first foetus arrives it will be layered in a double water bag that helps protect it as it travels down the birth canal, once that water bag breaks, the puppy will inhale its first breath, filling the lungs with water fluids from the bag and may drown. Always break the bag from the mouth down over its body if you are needed to assist with the whelp. The female will often lick and chew the bag around the puppy once it is born to rip it open so the puppy can take its very first breath. Your female should then also chew the cord, but assistance may be needed to help cut the cord with clean sterile scissors leaving approximately 1cm from the belly button. Even when the cervix if fully dilated, the exit out may still be too small for the puppy to exit, using lube you can apply plenty to the entrance of the vaginal walls to help make it easier for the puppy to slide from the exit. When the female is in labour you can help her by 'feathering' if you notice her contractions slowing down or not being strong enough. Feathering helps to stimulate contractions and is known to be as useful as using oxytocin. 'Feathering' is a term used when your feather the inside of the female's vagina in a 'come here' motion with plenty of lubricant and a glove. As you feather your female it will stimulate her to push down, you should be able to feel a puppy in the canal, that can be seen as a lump just under her bum as the puppy is ready to exit from the vagina. At this stage of labour your female should have calmed down from panting and concentrating more on her contractions and pushing. It is important to keep your female quite active in labour, offering regular lead walks around the garden to keep her bladder empty, if a female's bladder is full during labour, she can be also holding puppy's in. When she is pushing to urinate, she is also pushing a puppy down the birthing canal so keeping her active will help the labour progress. Be sure to take a towel with you outside when you take her to the toilet or on small walks in case she is to deliver a puppy outside, but do not worry if you see a puppy sack come down out of the vagina and then expel back up a few times with contractions, this is completely normal so do not try and pull it out or pop the sack, it will eventually slide out, however, you can help a puppy out if it is already there and becomes stuck by helping the puppy to a straight line position with your fingers to help ease a puppy out if a leg is tucked behind the puppy. This should only ever be done with the mothers' contractions as timing is crucial and you may only need to do this with the first puppy delivered as it will open the exit wider for the rest of the puppies to follow. Do not be anxious about taking over to help any puppies where needed if she is struggling, you can stimulate and dry the puppy by rubbing it all over with clean towels. Once a puppy has been delivered it should make loud crying/squealing noises, which is good, this helps the puppy to clear their own airways from any fluid that may have been ingested when the amniotic sac was broken. Your whelping mother may seem very rough with her new-born's, this is normal behaviour, she will lick them and flick them all around her whelping box during cleaning and stimulating them. As each puppy in the amniotic sac is delivered, your main priority is to get the puppy out of the sac within the first few minutes and stimulated, but it is also important to encourage the mother to do it herself as some people panic and do it instantly, not giving the mother a chance herself which helps with feeding and milk stimulation. With each puppy that has been delivered a placenta should follow closely behind, if a puppy is to exit with the placenta still attached inside the vagina, cut it as far away from the puppy as possible. The placenta may then retract back into the female, but do not worry as it will come out eventually whether it be before another puppy is delivered or after. The whelping mothers will eat placentas help keep her milk supply full and her uterus return to normal. Eating the placentas is fine to do so, but never let her overeat them, only a few will be sufficient as too many may make her sick, discarding the rest in a bag to the side and dispose of them before she can eat them. Nothing should be applied to the ends of the cords but instead with gloves on, clamping the ends between your fingers for a few seconds will stop and bleeding. If a puppy is to come out not breathing, lethargic, or full of fluid you may do the swinging motion method to help get air into the lungs and clear any mucus or fluid that the puppy may have ingested. Wrap the puppy up inside a warm clean towel with its head pointing upwards towards the ceiling, swing the puppy in a downwards position through your legs, repeat the process, and use a nasal aspirator to help suction the fluid away that has come up through the nose and mouth. The swinging motion method is well-known to help bring air into the lungs and make any fluid build-up run out of the mouth and nose, making space for the puppy to breathe air. In-between swinging, rub the puppy vigorously to help with stimulating the organs, do this until you can no longer hear, and fluid build-up on the puppy's chest. Afterbirths may not come out after each puppy is delivered, but instead come out in two's, ensure there is one placenta delivered per puppy born. Some females can become extremely ill and sick drastically if they have what is called a 'retained placenta,' where a placenta stays inside the female and does not come out in the process of labour. A female than has a retained placenta will need to see a vet immediately. A female that has needed to have a c-section will almost never get the chance to eat any placentas, but you can ask your vet to keep you some to feed her at home, so she is getting the goodness. As the puppies are born, her bedding will become soiled, wet, and full of discharge and fluids, you as the breeder should keep this clean and sterile, although it is hard to move the new mother and puppy's once the whelping has started. You can layer a new fresh clean blanket over the soiled mess as each puppy is born, then clean it all out properly once the labour is finished. Moving the mother and puppy's is easily done by having two people present, one takes the mother outside to toilet and distracts her, whilst the other person puts the puppies into a safe, warm box and cleans out the whelping area, providing fresh, clean bedding and a high protein meal. The whelping mother may be distressed if her puppies are moved away from her, be sure to have short toilet breaks only to keep the whelping mother content. Always leave the bedding flat but rugged, this is so the puppies are not easily covered up, but they can still strengthen their muscles by having grip to walk. Puppys need to be able to walk and manoeuvre around the whelping box freely because it helps prevent puppy swimmer's syndrome occurring, which is later explained. It is best to put the puppy's on to their mothers' nipples as often as you can when the mother is giving birth to help stimulate contractions. Knowing when your whelping female needs a vet's assistance is extremely important in the birthing process to ensure the safe arrival of puppies and the health and life of your female. Once a female in is the stages of pushing a puppy should be born within two hours of continuous pushing, although larger breeds can take a lot longer as the birthing canal is longer to get all the puppy's down. If you find it has been too long since the arrival of a puppy, then contact your vet who will advise what to do next and assist. If your female needs immediate vet assistance, they usually administer two shots of oxytocin thirty minutes apart to see if she needs the extra boost for stronger contractions, or it could be that she needs a c-section strait away. Long pauses are known in whelping dogs, especially larger breeds like germen shepherds and Dobermans, but too much of long pauses can cause death in puppy's that may be stuck or too big to exit the birthing canal, which blocks any puppies behind from being delivered. If some puppies have already been delivered by the time she needs to go to a vet, then you can take the puppies with you in a box with towels and a warm hot water bottle with you. C-section mothers sometimes become reluctant to feed their new-born puppies, often because she has not physically given birth to them, but be persistent and patient, with plenty of helping and assisting they will be thriving. Puppys born by c-section tend not to move around as much as puppy's delivered naturally because some anaesthetic from the surgery is transmitted to them. A caesarean section wound will not put a mother off feeding her puppies, but it is extremely important for you to clean the wound twice per day to prevent bacteria and infections, as well as making sure the stitches are healing as described by your vet. Stitches are usually taken out after ten or twelve days, after a health check on your female to ensure she is healing well and to speak about any concerns your may have. For the first twenty-four hours after your female has given birth, she will have a green discharge from her vulva, known as the lochia, as well as new and old blood for up to seven weeks after giving birth. Discharge should never have a foul-smelling odour or turn black; this is a sign of an infection and should be treated at a vet. It is important to keep the environment calm, cool and peaceful for the mother to whelp her puppies comfortably, ensuring no other dogs encounter her, even if they usually live and sleep together as it is likely to cause stress for the mother and cause her not to contract and go into labour. Once all the puppies have been delivered, the new mother will sleep deeply for some hours, giving the puppy's chance to have a good, settled feed and sleep too. Heat lamps or mats should be always turned on for the first two to three weeks of the puppy's lives as they can not regulate their own temperature. The new mother may be reluctant to go outside to toilet once the puppy's have been born, but you can use a slip-lead to get her out for slow walks around the garden.

Helping a puppy with feeding

With clean/sterile hands or gloves on, pick the puppy up comfortably and safely and move it towards the mother's teat/nipple, the puppy's head must be able to move around freely to find the nipple and latch on before putting it down gently with plenty of support. However, some puppies may struggle at first and may need some help from you by carefully pressing on the teat in a downwards position (like milking a cow) to encourage some milk to flow, slowly open the puppys mouth so it can get a taste, if needed you can wiggle the nipple around the puppys mouth area until it latches and is comfortable with sucking. Once the puppy has a taste of the milk, they will be able to smell it and make their own way to feed alone when they are hungry. Make sure the puppy is warm and never try to feed a puppy that is cold to the touch, it will need warming up. Sometimes puppies will latch on to the nipple immediately after being born, but with some it can take time, with persistence keep putting them onto the nipple to feed as often as possible at least every 2 hours or hourly if they need extra assistance. If you find you are still having problems getting the puppy/puppies to latch on to the mothers' nipples, contact your vet for help and advice before they become dehydrated and very poorly. Intervention with bottle feeding will be needed if they are not drinking and form of milk at all as soon as you notice a puppy struggling to latch on to the nipple you must intervene. Usually, puppys will struggle to latch if something is wrong like a cleft pallet or lip. The nipples towards the hind legs are always the ones that produce the most milk so it is best putting a puppy that may be struggling with suckling onto one of these rather than any others that produce milk slower until her milk is fully in and the puppys suction becomes stronger. If you notice a puppy that is cold or lethargic and is not attempting to suckle at all then it is suffering with fading puppy syndrome. All puppies should get as much as the mother's milk as they can in the first 12-24 hours of life as these are the most critical hours for puppy survival. A puppys GI epithelial lining is only open to antibody absorption for the first 24-48 hours of its life so colostrum, the first milk that will be produced from the mother is extremely important.

Puppy Development

Body temperature:

0-14 days old 34.4-37.2c

15-28 days old 36.1-37.8c

35 days old 38.3c (Adult temperature)

Respiration rate:

At Birth 12 breaths per minute.

7-35 days old 20-30 breaths per minute.

35+ days old 15-30 breaths per minute (Adult rate).

The birth weight of each puppy born in all breeds should double in 8-10 days.

Physical development of puppy's:

7-10 days eyes should open.

14-21 days primary teeth come through.

14 days the ear canals open.

Puppies should be wormed at 2 weekly intervals, starting at two weeks old until 12 weeks old, then every three months throughout there life. Some wormers can be administered monthly or three monthly, depending on the brand, always check the labels or ask for advice if you are unsure before administering. Some vets offer worming and flea packages that can be sent straight to your door when your dog is due to be wormed. Puppies until eight weeks old are wormed using a syrup or paste unlike a tablet once they are 10-12 weeks onwards, making it easier to digest without choking.

Puppy's can see their first sightings at 10-15 days old.

 Barking will start at around 18 days old.

Puppies should be standing upright by 21 days old.

Eating from a dish starts at 24-27 days old.

Puppy's sight is of an adult at 28 days old.

Playing development starts at 18-20 days old.

Playing with littermates from 25-28 days old.

Puppy's will urinate and defecate without stimulation at 21 days, once the puppies are at the weaning process.

Puppies will recognise and play with toys at 29-35 days old.

Hernias in dogs are more common than people think, especially in puppies. A hernia is a condition where the contents of a dog's abdomen push through a tear or hole in the fatty tissue or muscle wall, usually from straining, genetics, or the mother chewing on the cord at birth too far down that puppy's the muscles through the tissue. Over 90% of hernia cases are due to genetics, as most puppies are born with them, found near the belly button or abdomen area. Some hernias tent to go away in time on their own, but most will need surgery to repair the hole. There are many different types of hernias:

Umbilical hernias are the most seen hernias in dogs, effecting 90% of puppy's, making it genetical. Umbilical hernias appear as a soft swelling lump on the abdomen, usually near the belly button area, caused by when the fat from the abdomen enters the hole the umbilical cord passes through at birth. Usually, these types of hernias are nothing to be overly concerned about, but they can be dangerous if the bowel or any other organs exit through the hole. Umbilical hernias can be repaired with minor surgery, where the hernia is opened, fat removed from the muscle edges and skin, then closed to here. Sometimes if a hernia is large, they will put a special surgery mesh over the hole, which helps the muscle to heal over it better. Recovery usually takes 7-10 days, but exercise is restricted for up to one month, giving plenty of time to heal correctly.

Perineal hernias are swelling around the bottom, commonly seen in middle aged and older dogs from straining too much, especially seen in older male's (not neutered). It is thought to be due to straining, causing large prostate and muscle weakening. On occasion these hernias can trap the bladder or bowel, leading to symptoms of being unwell, vomiting and not being able to pass urine are the main symptoms. Perineal hernias should always be managed with surgery that will reconstruct the pelvis support muscle, as life threatening organ entrapment can occur if it is left a long period of time. Castration should also be done at the same time of the operation to reduce the risk of it happening again. Dogs that have had this surgery will often need to take stool softeners daily for the rest of their lives to reduce the need to strait when toileting. Swelling and bruising is common after both surgery's and two weeks crate rest is advised while the wounds are healing.

Inguinal hernias are seen in the groin area, where the hind leg attaches to the stomach area and are common in all breeds, especially older females. Inguinal hernias can often range in size and have high risks of trapping parts of the bladder, bowel, and womb, which can become life threatening. Surgery is used to correct both sides as they are commonly noted to effect both sides of the groin area. An incision wound should be healed after surgery within ten days, but crate rest is advised for two weeks to prevent tearing.

Diaphragmatic hernias are caused by a traumatic accident such as being hit by a car. The force of the/a trauma causes a tear in the muscle, separating the abdominal cavity and the thoracic cavity that contains the heart and lungs. This can cause the stomach, liver, and guts to enter the chest, causing difficulty when breathing as it is putting pressure on the lungs giving them less space to expand. Emergency surgery is needed immediately to save the dogs life by opening the abdomen and closing the hole/tear in the diaphragm, but this surgery can often come with huge risks, because of other traumas the dog may have experienced at the same time and must be stabilized before they can be anaesthetised. Dogs can not breathe on their own whilst under anaesthetic so ventilators, or the use of IPPV (manual compressions on the bag connected to the anaesthetic machine) are used to breathe for the dog. The surgery itself is a huge risk, if the dog survives without any complications and has an uncomplicated recovery, they can be back to normal after two to three weeks of crate rest because the chances of the tear re-opening is high. The dog may have lung damage, which causes blood and air to leak into the chest cavity that will need draining as well as a prolonged stay at the vet. The prognosis of recovery is high if they survive 48 hours after surgery.

A hiatal hernia is the protrusion of the upper part of the stomach into the chest cavity, through the oesophageal hiatus in the diaphragm (where the tube that carries food to the stomach passes through to the abdomen). This is rare in dogs and is usually a birth (congenital) defect in breeds like French bulldogs and pugs. Dogs with a hiatal hernia tent to vomit or regurgitate their food, due to the abnormal position of their stomach. French and British bulldogs are commonly known for this when they are too fast or get excited. Medical treatment is the go-to first before surgery, which includes acid reflux and stomach emptying medications. Surgery is only done in extreme cases by reducing the size of the hole in the diaphragm and stitching the stomach to a normal position.

Puppy defects, conditions, and abnormalities

A cleft palate is the condition in which both halves of the hard palate in the mouth do not fuse together as they should and causes an open roof of the mouth that can be physically seen on inspection. Cleft palates are most seen in short nosed breeds but can happen with all breeds. To detect a cleft palate, milk will be seen coming from the puppy's nose when feeding off the mother as there is no form of suction to draw the milk out correctly.

Depending of the severity of the cleft palate and how it will affect the puppy later in life, a vet will recommend them to be euthanized, or tube fed, with complications throughout the puppy's life, including surgery to close the hole.

A harelip is an inherited condition when the failure of the upper lip fails to join properly in the midline and is often seen with a cleft palate, which can be corrected with surgery. Id a puppy has both severe cleft palate and harelip they will be euthanised at birth. Puppy's will often be euthanised when both are severe because they would have poor quality of life, therefore health testing is especially important before breeding, to prevent the genes passing down to any offspring.

Open fontanel is a condition in which the bones do not fuse together properly to form the adult skull and instead leaves a hole, which can often lead to fluid on the brain if slightly knocked or injured leading to brain damage. This is most seen in smaller breeds like chihuahua's and are often advised by a vet to be euthanised because small knocks often cause major repeated damage. It is seen as though the puppy affected will not make it to adulthood without any knocks because of puppys playing and being exited, causes knocks to the head that cannot be helped.

Anasarca or 'water babies' are puppy's that are born with a generalised accumulation of water in their tissues, making them exceptionally large and abnormal due to the fluid build-up, enlarging the full body. Vets often advise putting a water puppy to sleep, but with plenty of care, observation and running your finger with a glove over the genital area to manually stimulate them to urinate could help save the puppy's life. A water pup has nothing to do with how much water a mother has drank during pregnancy but is believed to be low blood sugar (anaemic). There is no evidence that this condition is hereditary, but it does affect some breeds more than others, especially brachycephalic breeds (flat nosed). The choice to try and save a water puppy is between yourself and your vet and relies on how experienced or comfortable you are having this type of condition rely on you as a breeder. Breeders often feel down or left feeling like it is their fault if anything happens to the puppy, some conditions cannot be helped and are unexpected so anything you do try can only help in this situation. Most water puppy's pass away within the first week of being born, some are only two or three days old. My personal experience with this is plenty of time, effort, and persistence, a water puppy can go on to live a normal, health and happy life, even being on the larger scale of a water filled puppy. Keeping up with stimulating them to urinate is most important as well as warmth and feeding. Stimulating the genital area to urinate every twenty minutes will help rid the fluid.

Swimmers' syndrome is a condition seen more often in puppy's, which they are unable to walk or stand upright, but instead lies flat on its chest with its legs extended out to the sides. There puppies can only move in a swimming motion and often causes a flat chest, making it uncomfortable to breathe and in some cases unable to eat because they cannot stand up. Therefore, bedding in the whelping area should be flat but rugged, so the puppy has plenty of grip when learning to walk. Vet bedding is the best thing to have down in your whelping box, it is non-slip, washable and warm. Swimmer puppies often regurgitate their milk and end up with lifelong joint problems including deformities as they position their legs at abnormal angles for long periods of time. Puppy's that have swimmer's syndrome will have flat/flattened chests unlike the usual rounded chest, the puppy may have some difficulty breathing and breathe a lot shallower to the rest of the littermates, they are also seen as lethargic because they are unable to manoeuvre around the whelping box like the others. Smaller breeds are more likely to have swimmer's syndrome and not enough evidence suggests why it happens, some believe it is hereditary, but most people believe it is environmental factors like not being on the correct surface. Swimmers' syndrome if often treatable with homemade splints and physiotherapy by the breeder. You can make a 'H' shaped splint which can be used for up to four hours per day along with a sling type harness to keep as much pressure off the chest area as possible. You can also keep up with changing position of the puppy by alternative either side, so it is never laid on its chest. Avoid putting any puppies on slippery surfaces that encourage the legs to spread outwards, but you can also use two fingers as a support underneath them to gain strength in the leg muscles whilst they learn to walk.

Puppy's eyes usually open around day ten after they are born and can sometimes develop conjunctivitis before they even open, which is a plus-laden discharge from the corners of the eyes, usually caused by an infection under the eyelid. Conjunctivitis is extremely contagious in both humans and dogs and may be spread to the other littermates. The eyes can be kept clean by bathing them with a warm cotton pads and cool boiled water, wiping them every few hours. You can also help by opening the eye to let any fluid build up leak out as you wipe.

Hypoglycaemia, commonly known as low blood sugar and usually shows within the first three months of a puppy's life. This is a condition that is usually caused by lack of sufficient glucose stores in the body to sustain them through stressful events or fasting periods. This condition can also be caused by intestinal parasites or a physical abnormality involving the liver, which if left untreated it can cause seizures, coma, and death. Smaller breeds are particularly vulnerable to this condition because they have a higher metabolic rate. Physical signs and symptoms of this condition are weakness, shivering, seizures, stumbling, twitching, and shaking. When the blood sugar levels drop quickly, puppies cannot regulate their own temperature so they become cold and drowsy because of the lack of available sugar in the blood stream, effecting the nervous, which will always require a vet to take a CBC (complete blood count). You can supplement your puppy with honey on the gums until seen by a vet, or to help bring it out of an episode of seizures by administering a teaspoon of honey onto their tounge or rubbing it around the gums. A puppy diagnosed with hypoglycaemia will need to be managed through diet and medication for the rest of its life, as a breeder you are dependable for passing all background health information to a potential new owner. Some people can access their puppys record by the previous vet's emailing the relevant information over to the new one's directly.

Puppy strangles, also known as puppy head gland disease is a rare condition that comes on suddenly from three weeks to six months of age and can affect more than one littermate at a time. It is marked as a swelling of the muzzle, eyes, and face, leading most breeders to think the puppy has had a bite or been stung as the physical symptoms are very much the same. The lymph nodes of the throat become very enlarged leaving very little airway to breathe. This condition is regarded as idiopathic, meaning the condition is unknown, although some research has found that it does have an immune-meditated component that causes the immune system to attack its own skin. Juvenile cellulitis, as puppy strangles is also known as is likely to developing certain breeds like golden retrievers, dachshunds, and Gordon setters. Although puppy strangles is known to start on the face, it can also spread to the paws, anus, and vulva. Skin scrapings from your vet are usually performed to rule out mange and fungal cultures may be used to rule out ringworm, as mange and ringworm appear the same as juvenile cellulitis. Prednisone is usually prescribed by your vet over a seven-week period and does come with side effects such as an increased thirst and urination, as well as an increase in appetite.

Fading puppy syndrome is a condition that causes the puppy to die suddenly and unexpectedly, when the puppies have been healthy and thriving just hours before dying, so there is no exact cause of the death. It is never known if its something the breeder has done wrong and often blame themselves, when they have done everything correct and in fact nothing can be done. Puppies with puppy fading syndrome usually die within one to three weeks of being born and it is often quick, although scientists and vets have massively examined all aspects, but still never to prove a cause. Some factors that could contribute are poor maternal care, poor milk quality/lack of milk, inadequate immunity, intestinal parasites, bacterial infection, viral infections, low birth weight, birth defects and dystocia. Dystocia is when a female dog struggles when whelping to push a puppy out, the puppy is more likely to die being in the birth canal too long or be more fragile to puppy fading syndrome unlike than other puppys that have been delivered quicker. Puppies are also vulnerable to fading puppy syndrome if the mother is not taking to motherhood well. If a whelping mother has poor quality milk, she will be unable to fully nourish the puppy's, they become vulnerable and weak. Other threats like viruses and parasites can increase the risk of puppy fading syndrome as the immune systems of the puppys are undeveloped and can contract infections from the mother, especially if she is unvaccinated, or is carrying parvovirus, distemper, or adenovirus. It is extremely important for the puppies to latch onto their mothers' nipples soon after giving birth, because the special liquid called colostrum that they first feed on, fills them with nutrients that will boost their immune system and protect them until they are vaccinated. All puppies should receive this milk within twelve hours of being born, when the puppies intestinal lining absorbs the colostrum best. Puppies with fading puppy syndrome will often fail to thrive, the mother will help these puppies for a while, but them will let nature take its corse as there is nothing else, she can do. The first signs of fading puppy syndrome, you as the breeder can help by tube feeding every two hours, using life-drops, which stimulate the organs by administering a drop onto their tounge. You can also rub honey onto the puppy's gums for the sugar supply and most importantly keep them warm and manually stimulated to pass urine and faeces. Their poo will be watery/yellow. Once fading puppy syndrome symptoms are noticed, immediately get them to a vet where they will be administered aggressive care that includes fluid drips and IV antibiotics. Puppies will very rarely make it through the next few days, which can be very costly, resulting in breeders choosing to let nature run its corse rather than pay an extortionate amount of money with low survival rate. Research and personal experience have found that if one puppy in the litter is affected by fading puppy syndrome, then it's likely to pass through with litter, with a puppy fading every twenty-four hours. Keeping a puppy warm is the most important thing at the beginning of puppy fading syndrome, but it can be extremely dangerous if a puppy is heated too rapidly, it may cause seizures. Puppys that appear to have puppy fading syndrome should be separated in a box or incubator, away from the mother and non-effected puppies. If the puppy is becoming more energetic and lively them, it is acceptable to put her onto the mother to feed again. There are many ways to try and prevent puppy fading syndrome, but none of these are facts. Feeding a mother, a high-quality diet, having your vet do a culture would rule out e. Coli bacteria in the female's vagina before breeding, taking the mother and puppies to a vet soon after whelping to ensure their health. Taking a mother and puppies to a vet soon after whelping is something many breeders disagree on, taking a mother out of her area will cause her stress, it may be cold temperatures outside and puppys need to stay warm, vets' office also has potential risks of catching bacteria's and infections. A nice, comfortable, warm bed is what the mother needs, introduce her whelping box weeks before labour is due so she can adjust to it, no antibiotics are to be given to a whelping mother before or after the labour, unless a c-section had been performed as these can be transmitted to the puppy's whilst nursing, vets administer safe ones. Vets often advise the mother not to be bred from again if they have had several faders in the litter, as it is highly likely to happen again, but it is not known why it happens or how to prevent it. The clinical signs are very vague, and by the time these are recognised, it is often too late. Clinical signs of puppy fading syndrome can be physically seen in low birth weight, failure to gain weight, shallow breathing, decreased activity, failure to suckle on the mother's nipple, often crying out or being the loudest of the litter, lethargy, loss of muscle tone and they often crawl away from their littermates to be alone. Fading puppy syndrome is often missed by the breeder and often mistakenly known as the 'runt' of the litter. The runt of the litter is known as the smallest. Fading puppy syndrome causes the puppy to dehydrate dramatically, testing if a puppy is dehydrated by pulling up the skin at the back of the neck, if the skin stays up, or goes down slow, your puppy is dehydrated. Administering fluids by tube feeding for the best chances of survival once dehydration is seen.

Tube feeding is very easy, but should only be done in extreme circumstances, by a trained, confident person. First, you will need your supplies ready and prepared, which include a 12ml syringe, a soft rubber feeding tube, you can order packs online that will come prepacked for you. You will need a puppy replacer that contains goats' milk, weighing your puppys to monitor weight gain or loss, so you know if syringe or tube feeding is helping. For every ounce of the puppy's weight, you should be feeding the puppy 1ml of milk replacer. Preparing milk is simple, almost the same as making human baby milk, by boiling the kettle so the water is sterile, leave it to cool and mix with the milk replacer into a bottle and shake well until it forms to a milk, pull the milk up into the syringe, connect the syringe to the feeding tube and push the milk to the end of the tube so no air is pushed into puppy's stomach. Putting air into a puppy's stomach can cause bloating and gas pains that causes a puppy to be in pain and cry. Measure out the feeding tube by holding the end of the feeding tube at the belly button and feed the tube to the nose or mouth while the puppy is laid down, take the reading at the mouth, this is how far the tube will be inserted to avoid the lungs. Making sure the milk is not too hot, pour some onto your wrist to check the temperature. Gently clasp the puppy's head with your hand and put some milk into the puppy's mouth to coat the oesophagus before feeding. Tio the puppy's head slightly upwards whilst it is laid on a flat sofa surface using a blanket and slowly, but efficiently, feed the tube down the throat, putting the tube down too slowly will cause the puppy to gag. The puppy should start to make swallowing motions as the tube is being pushed into the stomach, which is a good sign the milk is filling the stomach and not the lungs. It at anytime the puppy starts to cough or gag, then pull the tube out and start the process again. Feed the tube down to the stomach, stopping at the measurement number on the tube you measured earlier from the belly button to the nose. After feeding the tube down into the puppy's stomach, push the syringe using a 3 second rule per 1ml of milk, by counting three seconds in your head for each ml administered, take a small pause after each ml to ensure no milk is coming up through the nose, which is a sign the puppy is chocking, the tube must ne removed immediately and any milk suctioned away with a nasal aspirator. Once the correct amount of milk has been fed, gently pull the tube out and let the puppy suck your finger (with a glove on), so it is less likely to be sick. If the mother is present and able after tube feeding, bring the puppy to her so she can stimulate it to toilet by licking the genital area to prevent constipation. Stimulating a puppy, yourself manually is quite easy using a glove and a baby wipe, wet cotton wool ball/pad, wipe the genital area gently, that will create the feeling of the mothers tounge. Stimulating a puppy after each feel will help remove anything that may be blocked in the intestines. You can also help to burp a puppy if there are signs of gas or air being trapped, the puppys belly will be firm to touch instead of soft if air is present. By putting the head of the puppy in your hands upright, with their body settled in your palm, rub and pat gently. Tube feeding should be done every two hours for the first five days and then every three hours. Never force a feeding tube down a puppy's throat, it should always slide down easily, if there is any resistance then always pull the tube out and start again.

Bottle feeding is a lot of hard work that takes time, patience, and effort. Bottle feeding/hand rearing is usually needed if a mother passes away, has no milk supply, is on medication that can be transmitted to puppy's or puppies are failing to suck and thrive. You will need artificial milk formula, 2 ml syringes, a puppy feeding kit, sterilising tablets/solution, cotton wool balls/pads and weighing scales. Milk formula tubs always have the feeding instruction guide on the side of the box, explaining how much and how often they should be fed, going off age and weight. Newborn puppy's up to seven days old need feeding every two hours, including during the night, it can be hard if the mother has had a large litter, you will need more than one set of hands. After the first week, you can start gradually reducing the timing of the feeds to three hours, and after four weeks they can be weaned onto puppy food/puppy mush. At six weeks of age your puppies should be fully weaned onto puppy food and no longer depending on the mother for milk. Hold your puppy in a natural feeding position, supporting their head, making sure their belly is towards the floor to prevent choking. Bring the bottle to the puppy's mouth so they can smell the milk, the puppy should them latch onto the teat as it would the mother's nipple and start to suck. Give the puppy regular breaks between feeding and only stop when the puppy rejects the milk by turning its head away to the side, meaning the puppy is full. If at any time whilst feeding you see milk coming from the nose, stop and wipe it clean, use a nasal aspirator to suction any excess milk and try again using a bottle with a smaller milk flow. Some feeding bottles come with no holes readymade, this leaves you to create a hole with pin pricks until you reach the flow needed for your puppys, you can always add more holes for a faster flow as they get older and need more. If your having problems you may try syringe feeding, the same process, but slowly syringing the correct amount into the mouth

Week 1- Milk feed every 2 hours.

Week 2-3- Milk feed every 3 hours.

Week 4- Milk feed every 4-6 hours, offer a small bowl of water and puppy mush.

Week 5- Feed wet puppy food in a bowl, fresh water to drink and supplement with bottle feeding if necessary.

Week 6- Puppy's should be fully weaned onto complete puppy food, fresh water, feed four times per day. Never leave a puppy unattended with a large, filled water bowl, it should always be just enough water in the bowl to drink to avoid any puppies from drowning.

It is especially important to ensure bottles and feeding equipment are sterilised before and after each use to prevent the spread of bacteria and infections. Wash all bottles and tears after each use in warm soapy water, using a bottle brush to clean smaller areas or places you can't reach, rinse them all well after under the tap with plain water. After washing the bottles, sterilise them using a solution or tablet, available to buy from any chemist. Leave them in the sterile solution for the recommended time instructed to do so on the packet and always rinse them off with clean warm water. If your puppy has a good suction, they will have no problem with bottle feeding.

Reproductive organs

The female's reproductive tract consists of the female genital organs including the mammary glands, ovaries, uterus, vagina, and the vulva, which are all located in the female's abdomen, ranging in different shapes and sizes. The mammary glands are located just outside of the abdomen, in two rows, running from the groin area to the chest. The right and left side of the ovaries are located behind the kidneys, which are connected to the uterus by small ducts, known as the oviducts. The uterus extends from the area behind the ovary, to the back of the abdomen, just in front of the pelvis. The uterus terminates at the cervix, which separates the uterus from the vagina. The vagina passes through the pelvis to the vulva, which is the external opening of the vagina. Ovaries are suspended from the top of the female's abdomen by a large ligament called the suspensory ligament. The oviducts are small tubes, which extend from the ovaries to the uterine horns. At the end of the oviduct nearest ovary, a funnel-like structure called the infundibulum catches the (ovum) when it is released from the ovary. The uterus of a female dog is shaped like a 'Y,' with the arms of the 'Y' being longer than the stem. The longer arms of the uterus are called the uterine horns, the shortened stem is the body. The uterine horns extend from each ovary and join to form the body of the uterus. When the female is pregnant, the foetuses are arranged in a row on both sides of the horns. The very tip of the 'Y' is where the cervix can be located. The walls of the uterus are lined with a vascular and glandular lining called mucosa, containing smooth muscle. The muscular parts of the uterus are called the myometrium, and the inner lining Is called the endometrium. The cervix contains a connective tissue and muscle that forms a firm tube-like sphincter, which during fertilization and birth, the sphincter is relaxed or opened. The cervix is usually always closed to prevent the female from any infections. The vagina is exceptionally long and passes through the pelvis, towards the vulva, in a female that's 30lbs for instance, the vagina averages 18cm long and 1.8cm in diameter. Both the length and diameter increase during pregnancy and birth. The vaginal walls are made up of an inner muscular layer, a middle smooth layer, and an external layer of connective tissue. The vaginal mucosa contains numerous folds, which makes it easier when the whelping mother is giving birth because these layers stretch, creating a larger exit space for the puppies. Mammary glands are composed of connective tissue to provide support and structure, blood vessels, lymphatic vessels, and glandular tissue. Mammary glands contain small sac-like glands that store milk, which the milk eventually travels down through a duct system to empty the milk through the nipples.

Functions of the reproductive tract

The vagina provides a passageway from the outside of the body to the uterus, where the semen from a male dog is deposited through mating or artificial insemination during breeding. The vagina also provides a protective passage for puppys to exit out into the world, but also protects the urethra from infections, where the urine is passed through. The vulva protects the opening of the vagina and how we identify male and females apart. The function of the mammary glands is to provide milk for any future offspring. The ovaries contain the eggs that are waiting to be fertilised during a season/ ovulation, which also produce hormones of progesterone and estrogen. The eggs for fertilisation are released from small sac-like structure called follicles during the process of ovulation and pass through the fallopian tubes into the uterus. When a female dog has been spayed, the ovaries, oviducts and uterus are removed, and no eggs can be released. The main function of the uterus is reproduction as it serves as the site for implantation of fertilised eggs and for the growth and development of the foetuses. The uterus houses the fetus until it is ready to be delivered.

Disorders of the canine uterus

Pyometra is an inflammation and infection inside of the female's womb, where it fills with pus from a bacterial infection, which has travelled from the uterus. Hormonal changes during a season/heat can put your female at risk of a womb infection is not spayed. Once a female's season is over and finished, majority of dogs return to normal, but unfortunately, some females develop complications including pyometra, often knows as 'pyo.' If pyometra is left untreated it can lead to blood poisoning, kidney failure, peritonitis, and even death. Pyometra is a profoundly serious infection and must be treated immediately from a vet as soon as symptoms appear. Pyometra is either open or closed. An open pyometra is when the womb entrance is open, meaning blood and puss will be visible coming from the vulva. A closed pyometra is when the womb entrance is closed, meaning you are unlikely to see any visible symptoms. A closed pyometra is much more serious because it is at risk of bursting, because you can not see the physical signs in the early stage and may be now life threatening. Although exceedingly rare, occasionally a neutered dog will develop a specific type of pyometra, called a stump pyometra. After neutering a small womb stump remains inside your dog, that eventually develops an infection inside that stump. Ovary hormones are needed for stump pyo to develop, which means at the time of your females spaying, they have left a small piece of ovary tissue still inside, which has gone unnoticed at the time of the spay. For a dog to live, this will unfortunately have to be removed by another surgery. Pyometra can not be treated with medications or antibiotics alone, but for the womb to be removed as the only option. Your female will need plenty of crate rest and support, no jumping, running, or playing, and administer prescribed medications accordingly. The female will also need to wear a neck cone or protective surgery suit to stop them from licking the wounds. The only prevention from pyometra is having your female spayed when younger, keep a close eye out for signs and symptoms, which will appear four to eight weeks after their season. Signs of pyometra are drinking more than usual, vomiting, puss leaking from her vulva, a bloated abdomen, panting or weakness, not eating, urinating more than usual or they may collapse.

Metritis is the inflammation of the uterus and usually happens after pregnancy, when a bacterial infection ascends the vagina and gains entrance to the uterus through the open cervix. Uterine prolapse is the protrusion of the uterus, through the cervix, into the vagina. Portions of the uterus may be exposed at the vulva but is usually an uncommon condition. Uterine prolapse usually happens during or immediately after birth, with the delivery of the last puppy and can also be seen with a spontaneous abortion. Tumors may develop in the uterus, which can develop as both benign and malignant. Spaying/removal of the uterus prevents the development of uterine tumors.

Disorders of the canine vagina

Vaginitis is an inflammation of the vagina, which may occur at any age, nut juvenile vaginitis is seen in dogs less than one year old and often resolves after the first estrus cycle. Other causes for vaginitis include urinary tract infections, congenital defects, bacterial and viral infection, vaginal tumors, and vaginal trauma. Usually, the first signs of most of these infections are vaginal discharge. Vaginal hyperplasia or edema is an exaggerated response by the vaginal tissue to estrogen during certain phases of the heat cycle, where the vaginal tissue becomes swollen, and may be seen protruding through the vulva, in a donut shaped mass. Vaginal hyperplasia is most seen in young, intact females and is more common in boxers, English bulldogs, German shepherds, and certain other breeds, but it is varied. Tumors may develop in the vagina, particularly one called transmissible venereal tumor (TVT), which is a condition easily spreadable and contagious, often spread through breeding.

Disorders of the canine mammary gland for milk production include galactorrhea -milk production that is not associated with a pregnancy, agalactia- the failure secrete milk at appropriate times, and galactostasis- the abnormal collection of milk in the mammary glands. Mastitis is an inflammatory and/or infection of the mammary glands and is caused by bacteria traveling up the mammary ducts and into the glands, which become swollen, red, painful, and sore. Mammary gland tumors are the most seen tumors to develop in female dogs, especially females that have not been spayed. Mammary gland tumors are usually malignant, although some do not behave aggressively.

There are many ways of testing to evaluate the female's reproductive tract to detect infections, tumors, and health conditions like x-rays of the abdomen are useful in identifying enlargement of the uterus. If the ovaries and uterus is of normal size, they usually do not show up on a plain x-ray. A complete blood count, organ profile, urinalysis, and urine culture are often carried out to detect infections or other organ related abnormalities (e.g., bladder infections and kidney disease). Chest x-rays may be used if a tumor is present to detect metastasis. Vaginoscopy is an examination of the vulva and vagina, by putting a scope through the external genitalia, directly into the vagina to examine the area for tumors and inflammation. Vaginal cytology can be performed by retrieving cells of the vagina using a sterile cotton swab and examining the smears under the microscope. Vaginal cytology is extremely helpful in identifying where a female is at in their season as explained previously, but also detects infections. Cytology can also be performed on milk samples to identify infections. Ultrasonography of the abdomen is helpful in evaluating the internal organs with the use of high frequency waves. This can identify organ changes that do not show up on an x-ray, also used to identify pregnancy is females. Bacterial culture and sensitivity testing, by using a special culture swab or collection tube. These samples are collected, and attempts are made to grow the bacteria to identify them. If the bacteria are identified, several types of antibiotics are then used to determine which works best and is more suitable to kill the infection. A fine needle aspirate and examination of the cells is often useful when assessing masses or tumors. Biopsy of masses and abnormal tissue may also be performed. Removal of the organ affected and submitting it for a biopsy may be needed to identify the underlying problem and its cause.

After visiting a vet people are often left confused or unable to take in what they have said because of technical terms used which people don't understand. I have written a dictionary explaining technical terms and what the mean. The book can be used to take to a vet with you so words can be looked at and understood or researched at home.

Afterbirth- the membranes (placenta) expelled with each puppy during and after whelping.

Agalactia- the absence of milk. No milk producing from the nipples.

Allantois- the inner membrane surrounding the fetus in the uterus, part of the placenta.

Amnion- the outer membrane surrounding the fetus in the uterus, part of the placenta.

Anaerobes- bacteria which likes to grow in the absence of air and may occur in the uterus.

Anoestrus- the period of sexual inactivity in the oestrous cycle.

Benign- non-malignant, recurring or spreading, usually applied to a tumor or the mammary gland.

BHS- beta-haemolytic streptococci, round shaped bacteria which may cause vaginitis and be associated with fading puppy syndrome.

Biopsy- a minor operation to take away part of an effected tissue to diagnose the cause of the lesion and give it a prognosis.

Blastocyst- a specific stage in the development of the fetus, a type of embryo.

Broken-down- a term often used when females have coma on heat/started a season.

Brucellosis- the disease caused by an infection with the bacterium brucella canis.

Bursa- a sac-like structure, made usually of connective tissue. The ovary of a female is enclosed in a bursa.

Carcinogenic- cancer forming/producing.

Carcinoma- a type of malignant tumor.

Cervical- related to the cervix or the neck of the uterus.

Chorion- the outermost layer of the foetal membranes.

Coitus- sexual intercourse.

Colostrum- the first milk produced after giving birth.

Conceptus- offspring during development, embryo, or fetus.

Congenital- present at birth.

Cytology the examination of cells under a microscope.

Diapedesis- the passing of blood cells through the walls of intact blood vessels into the adjoining tissues.

Dys- a prefix meaning painful of difficult.

Dystocia- a difficult or abnormal birth.

Ecbolic- an agent that makes the uterus contract.

Ejaculation- expulsion od semen through the urethra to the outside.

Embryo- a developing puppy in the uterus, up to the time when the major organs are developed.

Endocrine glands- glands that secrete hormones into the blood to act as chemical messages.

Endometritis- inflammation of the womb lining.

Endometrium- the lining of the womb.

Episiotomy- incision of the vulva during whelping to avoid excessive laceration and trauma to the genital tract.

Fertilization- the fusion between the semen and the egg.

Fits- episodes of involuntary muscle spasms.

Fetus/Foetus- a developing puppy in the uterus from the time when the major organs develop until birth.

Follicle- a developing egg in the ovary.

FHS- follicle stimulating hormone- produced by the anterior pituitary gland in the brain, a gonadotrophin.

Gestation- period if development of the progeny in the womb, from fertilisation to birth.

Haematology- examination of the blood.

Haematoma- a mass of blood that has leaked from the blood vessels that become trapped under the skin or within a tissue.

Hermaphrodite- an animal that that had both one testical and one ovary.

Heat- a term used to describe pro-oestrus and oestrus.

Hepatitis- inflammation of the liver.

Heredity- the process of passing traits and behaviour from one generation to the next.

Histology- microscopic anatomy, looking at tissues under a microscope.

Hormone- a chemical messenger produced by and endocrine gland and transported in the blood to a target organ where it will exert its effect.

Hyper- a prefix meaning excessive.

Hyperplasia- excessive growth of a tissue.

Hypo- a prefix that means deficient or less of e.g., Hypothyroid- un underactive thyroid resulting in reduced levels of thyroid hormones in the blood.

Hypertrophy- increase in the size of a tissue or organ.

Hypoplasia – incomplete development.

Hypothalamus- an area in the brain, near the pituitary gland which produces a releasing factor that stimulates the production of FSH and LH.

Hypothermia- lowered body temperature.

Hysterectomy- surgical removal of the uterus.

Iatrogenic- caused my medication.

Idiopathic- an unknown cause.

Implantation- attachment of the embryo to the uterus before the placenta is developed.

Insemination- the placement of semen in the vagina through natural mating or artificial insemination.

Intramuscular- into the body of a muscle viz. Intramuscular injection, to inject into the site of a muscle.

Intravenous- into a vein viz. intravenous injection.

Intromission- the entrance of the penis into the vulva.

Involution- the decrease in size of an organ e.g., the uterus after giving birth.

Larva- an immature stage in the development of some parasites viz Toxocara canis.

Lesion- a pathological change in a tissue.

LH- luteinizing hormone, a gonadotrophin produced by the anterior pituitary, which brings about ovulation.

Lumen- the cavity in a hollow organ.

Malignant- severe, life threatening, capable of spreading.

Mastitis- inflammation of the mammary gland.

Melaena- black faeces due to digested blood.

Metasteses- tumors resulting from malignant cells spreading into other parts of the body.

Met oestrus- the stage of the oestrus cycle, which follows heat and precedes anoestrus.

Metritis- inflammation of the uterus.

Mis mating- an unwanted mating, unintentional.

Monoestrus- relates to the oestrus cycle and is applied to animals that only ovulate once per breeding season.

Morula- an embryo which consists of undifferentiated cells, incredibly early in its development.

Mucoid- a discharge that is like mucus. A clear, slimy, often tenacious fluid produced by a mucus membrane.

Necropsy- a post-mortem or autopsy.

Necrosis- a death of a tissue.

Neonatal- new-born.

Neoplasia- formation of a neoplasm or growth (tumor).

Oestrus- the period during the heat when the female will accept the male to mate.

Ovariohysterectomy- surgical removal of the uterus and womb - to spay.

Ovulation- the release of an egg from the ovary.

Ovum- an egg.

Oxytocin- a hormone produced by the posterior pituitary gland, which causes the uterus to contract during birth, which stimulates milk production. Often given as an injection.

Paediatrics- medicine relating to young animals.

Palpitation- examined by touch.

Parturition- the process of giving birth, whelping in the case of females.

Pathogenesis- the development of a disease process.

Perinatal- the period around the time of birth.

Perineum- the area around the anus, stretching to the vulva in females and to the scrotum in male dogs.

Physiology- the science in dealing with the function of organs.

Pituitary gland- an endocrine gland that lies on the underside of the brain.

Placenta- afterbirth.

Poly- a prefix meaning many or increased.

Polydipsia- Increased thirst.

Polyuria- passing urine more often and increased amounts.

Prognosis- the expected outcome of a disease.

Prolapse- protrusion, to the outside.

Pro-oestrus- the first stage of heat, when a female comes in season.

Prophylaxis- prevention of a disease.

Pseudocyesis- synonymous with pseudo or false pregnancy.

Puberty- the time of live when an animal becomes sexually mature.

Puerperal- the period after giving birth.

Pyrexia- raised body temperature, a fever.

In season- a lay term when a female is in heat.

Spay- surgical sterilisation of the female by the removal of the ovaries and uterus.

Staphylococci- bacteria which commonly occur, associated with skin diseases.

Subclinical- applied to a disease in which the signs are not obvious by clinical examination.

Subcutaneous- under the skin viz. subcutaneous injection.

Superficial- on the surface. Often applied to an open wound.

Syndrome- a set of signs which occur together indicating a particular condition or disease.

Tenesmus- painful and ineffective straining to pass faeces or urine.

Teratogenic- capable of producing abnormalities in puppy's whilst they are in the womb, applied to medicine e.g., Thalidomide.

Tie- the time in which the male dog's penis is held in the vagina during ejaculation.

Tissue- an aggregation of similar cells in the body, a muscle.

Toxaemia- the spread of bacterial products (toxins) in the blood from a source of infection.

Transplacental- transfer across the placenta from mother to puppy's e.g., the passage of infection or antibodies.

Trauma- injury, trauma, shock.

Tumor/Tumour- a growth, neoplasm.

Umbilical cord- the stalk of a blood vessel and other tissues which join the developing fetus to the placenta.

Umbilicus- the point on the abdominal wall where the umbilical cord emerged.

Uterus- the womb.

Whelp- the process of the female giving birth to her puppies.

Zoonosis- a disease that can be transmitted from animals to human.

Printed in Great Britain
by Amazon

18120770R00041